LITTLE CARS
AND TRUCKS
Activity Book

Becky Radtke

DOVER PUBLICATIONS, INC.
Mineola, New York

Bibliographical Note

Little Cars and Trucks Activity Book is a new work, first published by Dover Publications, Inc., in 2007.

International Standard Book Number

ISBN-13: 978-0-486-45685-0
ISBN-10: 0-486-45685-4

Manufactured in the United States by LSC Communications
45685406   2019
www.doverpublications.com

Show this truck the way to get to the Recycling Center at the end of the path.

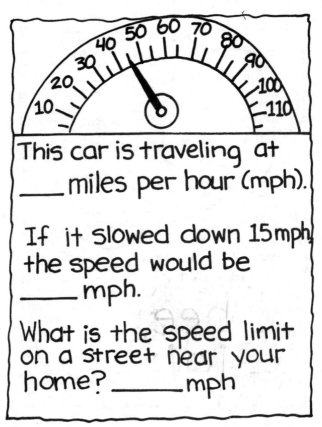

This car is traveling at _____ miles per hour (mph).

If it slowed down 15 mph, the speed would be _____ mph.

What is the speed limit on a street near your home? _____ mph

The picture at the top shows how fast a car is going. Use the picture to fill in the blanks.

___ teel

___ hingles

___ heetrock

___ iding

Find one letter of the alphabet that will spell four words that tell what the truck might be carrying.

Draw a line from each word on the left to a word on the right to name four things found on cars and trucks.

e _ gs
g _ apes
s _ up
ju i _ e
m _ eat
c _ ackers
m _ lk
l _ ttuce
chee _ e

Write the word **groceries** in the boxes from top to bottom.
You will spell nine things that the truck carries.

9

Use the number code to spell out a word used to describe older cars that are worth a lot to some people.

Solve the subtraction problems and write the numbers on the race car doors. Start your engines!

See how many new words you can spell using the letters in "limousine." You can write more words on a separate paper.

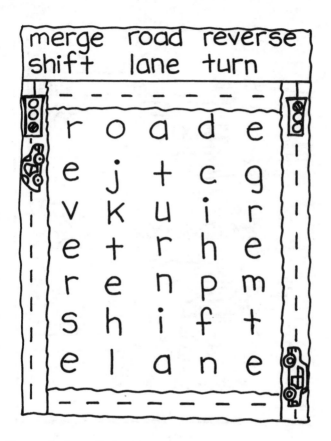

| merge | road | reverse |
| shift | lane | turn |

```
r o a d e
e j t c g
v k u i r
e t r h e
r e n p m
s h i f t
e l a n e
```

Six words that tell about driving are at the top of the page.
Find and circle them in the puzzle. Look up, down, and
across.

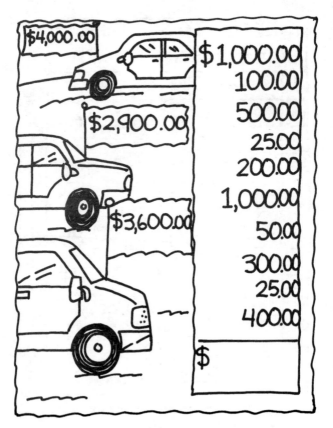

$4,000.00

$1,000.00
100.00
500.00
25.00
200.00
1,000.00
50.00
300.00
25.00
400.00

$2,900.00

$3,600.00

$

Ben wants to buy a used car. Add up the numbers to find out how much money Ben has. Then put a check on the car with that amount.

When you get ready...
To take a ride —
Make sure you're
    Wearing this,
When you're seated inside!

Cross out the first letter. Then cross out every other letter.
Write the letters that are left in order in the blanks to see
what the poem is about.

This driver is in a hurry! Count how many times he has honked his horn, and write the number in the traffic cone at the bottom.

16

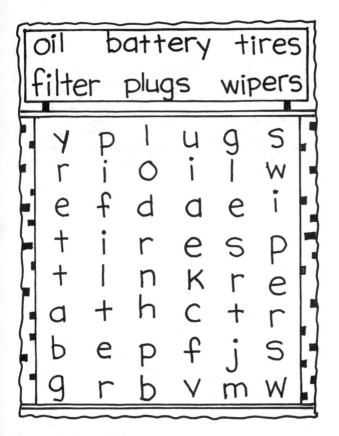

o i l	b a t t e r y		t i r e s		
f i l t e r	p l u g s		w i p e r s		

y	p	l	u	g	s
r	i	o	i	l	w
e	f	d	a	e	i
t	i	r	e	s	p
t	l	n	K	r	e
a	t	h	c	t	r
b	e	p	f	j	s
g	r	b	v	m	w

Six words that tell about cars are at the top of the page. Find and circle them in the puzzle. Look up, down, and across.

Look carefully at this picture. Circle the four things that Angie needs to wash her truck.

Color this bumper car, using the letter code at the top of the page. It's so much fun to drive one!

✓ It has only one story.
✓ The windows have shutters.
✓ It has double doors.
✓ It has bushes in front.

Oh, no! The truck driver has lost the address. Use the clues to help him find the right house. Draw a circle around it. +

Here are three drivers and three cars or trucks. Draw a line from each driver to his or her vehicle.

Cars and <u>trucks</u> are cool! They come in all <u>shapes</u> and <u>sizes</u>. They are <u>awesome</u>! Most people use this kind of <u>transportation</u> every day of the week. What do <u>you</u> hope to drive in the future?

Read the paragraph above. Then use the underlined words to do the puzzle on the next page.

Write each underlined word where it belongs in the puzzle.

Each pair of letters in the flags at the top can be added to the letters below to spell a car color. Write the letter pairs where they belong in the blanks.

24

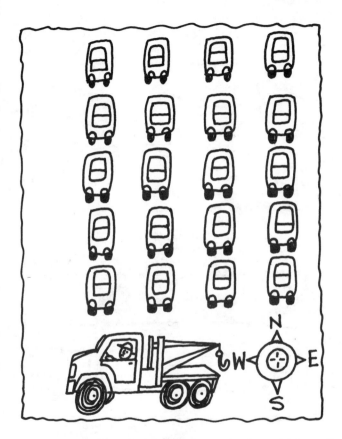

One of these cars called for a tow truck—but which one?
Starting at the lower left, go north three cars, east two
cars, and south two cars.

Each tanker truck carries something different. Fill in the blanks with the missing vowels to spell out these items.

Use the shape code at the bottom to solve the riddle.
You'll be surprised at the answer!

Here's a sporty car! Finish drawing the middle and bottom cars so that they look just like the top one.☐

Connect the dots and you will find out what kind of vehicle Greg saw at the Mud Rally.

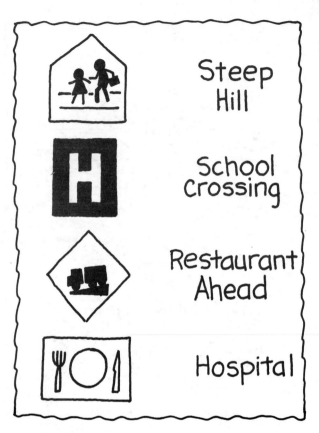

Steep
Hill

School
Crossing

Restaurant
Ahead

Hospital

Draw a line from each of the traffic signs on the left to its meaning on the right.

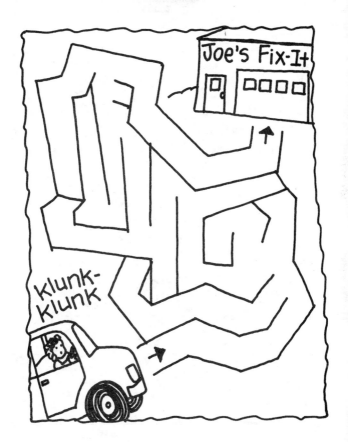

Uh, oh! Jasmine's car is breaking down! Show her the path to take to get to Joe's Fix-It shop.

José's friends have stopped by to see his new car.

This picture of José and his friends looks the same, but it's not. Find and circle six things that are different.□

Add the number of miles that Jan and Stan drove to get to their favorite restaurant. Circle that number in the window.

Here are five shiny, new pickup trucks. Look carefully and circle the two trucks that are exactly the same.

MR1DRFUL	I love tennis
AQT4EVR	A great lady
ILUV10IS	A cutie forever
AGR8LDY	Mister Wonderful

The letters and numbers on each license plate are another way of saying a group of words on the right. Draw a line from each plate to its meaning.

Here's your chance to make up your own license plate.
Decide what it would look like and draw it here!

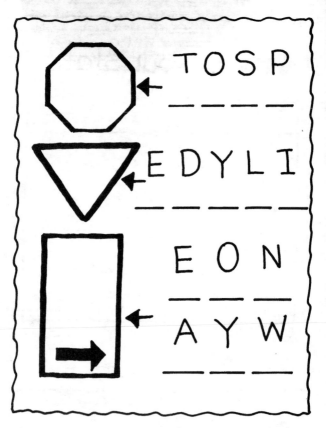

Unscramble the mixed-up words on the right and write them in the blanks. Then write them inside the signs at the left. 7

The Martins are carrying their things on moving day.
Find and color the hidden letters in the picture that spell
TRUCK./

Ethan has found four things wrong with his father's new car. Can you find all four things and circle them?

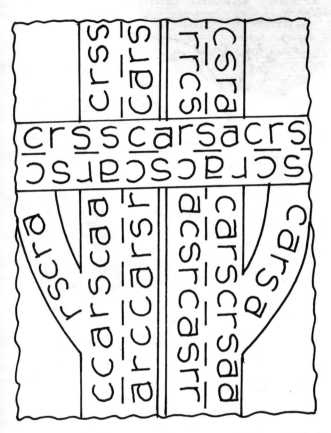

Here's a view from the air of a very crowded road. Find the word "cars" seven times and circle it each time.

↑ ↑ ↑ ↑ ↑ ↑ ↑ ↑ ↑

c d e q n r s d q

In each blank, write the letter that comes after the one shown. You will find out what you must turn on to melt the ice on your windshield.

42

Marissa's sister has just passed her driver's test! Show her the path to take to pick up her new license.h

Here are some dune buggies on the beach. Match each dune buggy to its shadow by writing the correct letter in the blank.

44

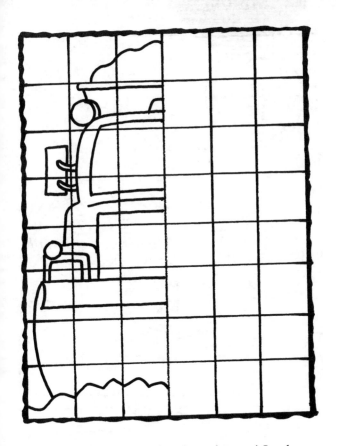

The truck with the snowplow is on its way! Look carefully at the picture and draw the other half of the truck.

Write each letter on the tires in the correct number order below. You will learn what a driver should always have.

46

How many...
Rectangles? _____
Circles? _____
Triangles? _____
Squares? _____

This ice cream truck is covered with shapes. Look at the truck and then answer the questions.

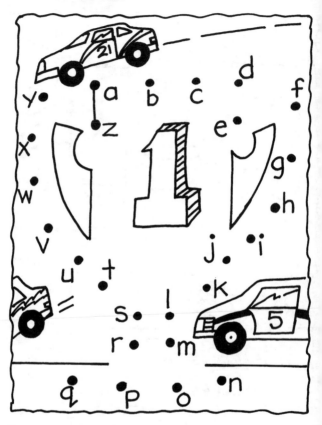

Connect the dots in alphabetical order to see the prize for the winner of this race.

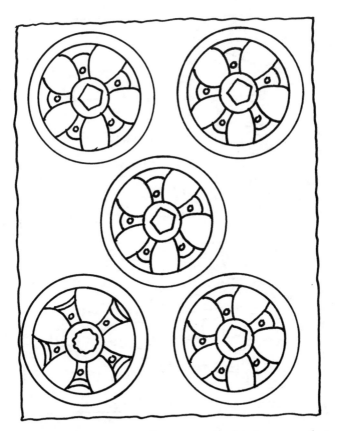

Here are five hubcaps. They seem to be the same, but they're not. Put an X on the hubcap that is different from the others.

Using the vowels at the top, fill in the empty boxes to spell three kinds of trucks.

odho ＿ ＿ ＿ ＿

ordo ＿ ＿ ＿ ＿

i r o r m r ＿ ＿ ＿ ＿ ＿ ＿

i e t r ＿ ＿ ＿ ＿

h i s l t g ＿ ＿ ＿ ＿ ＿ ＿

m p u r b e ＿ ＿ ＿ ＿ ＿ ＿

A car has many parts. Unscramble the mixed-up words and write the names of the car parts in the blanks.

Solutions

Page 5

This car is traveling at **45** miles per hour (mph).

If it slowed down 15mph the speed would be **30** mph.

What is the speed limit on a street near your home? **(will vary)** mph

Page 6

s teel
s hingles
s heetrock
s iding

Page 7

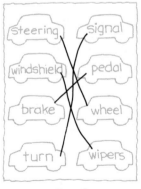

steering — wheel
signal — brake
windshield — wipers
pedal
turn — signal
wheel

Page 8

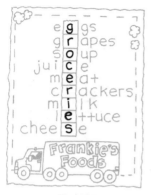

Page 9

eggs
grapes
soup
juice
meat
crackers
milk
lettuce
cheese

Frankie's Foods

Page 10

5=s 2=l
3=a 7=c
1=c 6=i
4=s

c l a s s i c
1 2 3 4 5 6 7

Page 11

13 - 6 = 7
19 - 9 = 10
7 - 3 = 4

Page 12

limousine

(possible answers)	
lion	lime
men	nose
smile	oil
mouse	line
lemon	mule

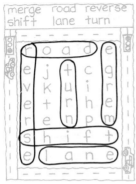

Page 13

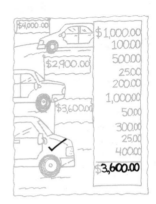

Page 14

Page 15

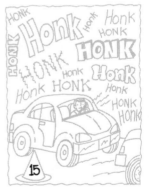

Page 16

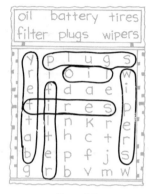

Page 17

Page 18É

Page 20

✓ It has only one story.
✓ The windows have shutters.
✓ It has double doors.
✓ It has bushes in front.

Page 21

Page 23

Page 24

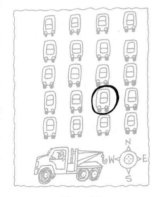

Page 25

Page 26

Page 27

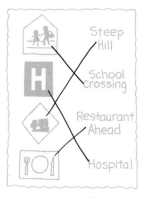

Page 29

Page 30

Page 31

Page 33

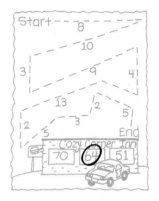

Page 34≤

Page 35

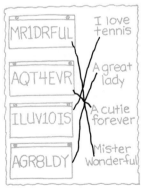

Page 36

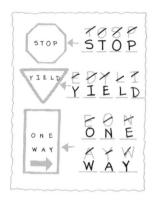

Page 38

Page 39

Page 40

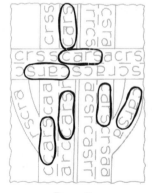

Page 41

Page 42

Page 43

Page 44

Page 46

A S P A R E
1 2 3 4 5 6

How many...
Rectangles? __2__
Circles? __4__
Triangles? __2__
Squares? __3__

Page 47

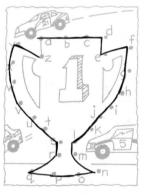

Page 48

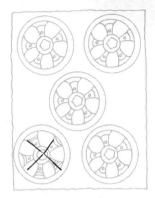

Page 49§

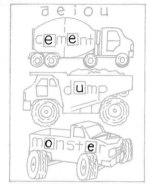

Page 50

Page 51